BIRD

PETS WE LOVE

Lynn Hamilton and
Katie Gillespie

www.av2books.com

Step 1
Go to **www.av2books.com**

Step 2
Enter this unique code

AWOIF9INM

Step 3
Explore your interactive eBook!

CONTENTS

AV2 is optimized for use on any device

Your interactive eBook comes with...

Contents
Browse a live contents page to easily navigate through resources

Audio
Listen to sections of the book read aloud

Videos
Watch informative video clips

Weblinks
Gain additional information for research

Try This!
Complete activities and hands-on experiments

Key Words
Study vocabulary, and complete a matching word activity

Quizzes
Test your knowledge

Slideshows
View images and captions

... and much, much more!

PETS WE LOVE

BIRD

Contents

Feathery Friends

Birds are unique creatures. Their ability to fly has long been envied by humans. However, people also admire birds for their grace and singing skills. These are just a few of the reasons why people have kept birds as pets for thousands of years.

There are many different shapes and sizes of birds. They are cheerful with their whistling and chattering. It can be fun to watch them hop and flutter around. Some birds enjoy being held, petted, or cuddled.

Birds do not take up much space. They are quite intelligent and easy to train. A bird can be a nice choice of pet for people with allergies to cats or dogs. It is important to pay attention to your pet's needs. Birds require care every day to stay comfortable and healthy.

Birds come in a variety of colors, from dull brown or gray to bright blue or red.

There are more than
20 million
pet birds in the
United States.

Parakeets are the
most popular
pet bird species.

Pet macaws can live to be
65 years old.

There are about **10,000** species of birds on Earth.

The **goose** was the **first** bird to be **tamed** by humans.

The **myna** is bird that has been sacred in **India** for more than **2,000 years**.

The **archaeopteryx** lived **150 million** years ago.

Native peoples in the North American Southwest bred macaws for their feathers as early as 900 AD.

Bird Beginnings

The oldest bird ever found is the archaeopteryx. Many scientists believe that modern birds are descended from this ancient creature. In the United States, **fossils** of birds have been found dating back 90 million years. Over time, these animals became more like the birds we know today. Stronger wings and muscles were developed, and their skeletons became better suited to flying.

Some of the first animals ever **domesticated** by people were birds. In 2,000 BC, the Chinese raised falcons. They were trained to catch rabbits and pheasants for the emperor to eat.

Parakeets are a type of small parrot that can be trained to talk.

Starting in the early 1900s, miners would also use canaries to identify dangerous gases. If a canary stopped singing when sent into the mine, the workers knew it was unsafe to be inside. During World War II, canaries were used by soldiers. They would send the birds into tunnels behind enemy lines. It was the canary's job to detect poisonous gas that could be harmful to the soldiers.

Pet Profile

Each **breed** of bird has special features and behaviors. Their needs may vary, but every pet bird is dependent on its owner. When choosing a pet bird, consider the different characteristics of each breed. Like many large birds, parrots can be demanding. Canaries and finches need less attention. This has made them popular pet choices. Understanding the traits of each type of bird will help you choose the best fit for your family.

Cockatiels

- Have an average life span of 6 to 15 years
- Are usually white, gray, yellow, or brown
- Can be easily trained
- Are friendly birds
- Enjoy being held and cuddled
- Use **crests** on their heads to communicate with other birds
- Able to talk and whistle tunes

Doves

- Have an average life span of 12 to 15 years
- Are often gray, white, or brown in color
- Often make soft cooing noises
- Like to be kept warm
- Enjoy being held
- Are easily tamed
- Can grow even bigger than a chicken
- Are strong fliers

Conures

- Have an average life span of 10 to 25 years
- Come in many colors and sizes
- Are very active and playful
- Love to play with toys, but may destroy them
- Make loud, screechy noises
- Can be expensive
- May not be a good fit for children
- Enjoy being petted
- Require a large cage

Lovebirds

- Have an average life span of 10 to 15 years
- Have green feathers with different colors on their heads and tails
- Require time outside of their cage
- Are extremely social birds
- Do best with a companion
- Despite their name, may not always get along

Parakeets

- Have an average life span of four to eight years
- Come in many colors, such as blue, green, and yellow
- Are extremely friendly
- Can also be called budgerigars
- Are very talkative birds
- Learn well from children's voices
- Are affectionate and loving

Canaries

- Have an average life span of 10 to 15 years
- Are usually yellow, but can be other colors
- Can be left on their own
- Are talented singers (especially males)
- Some are messy eaters
- Have a good-natured temperament
- Do not enjoy being handled

There are about **308** species of **pigeons** and doves.

The **California condor** is the largest bird in North America, with a wingspan of more than **9 feet**. (3 meters)

Peregrine falcons are the **fastest** birds on Earth. They can dive at speeds of **240 miles** (386 kilometers) per hour.

Many birds can be trained to step up onto their owners' hands or shoulders.

Picking Your Pet

There are many factors to consider when buying a pet bird. To make the right choice for both you and your pet, think about the following questions.

What Can I Afford?

There are many expenses involved in owning a pet. You must buy your bird a cage and cover, so she has a place to live. Also important are accessories for your bird's cage, such as stands, swings, and **perches**. Birds need food to eat and toys to play with. You must also pay **veterinary** costs to keep your bird healthy.

Will a Bird Be Able to Rely on Me?

It is very important to take care of your bird and her needs. Birds are social creatures. Daily visits will keep your bird happy. If she is feeling ignored, your bird may act out. She might destroy items in her cage, or pluck out her feathers to get your attention. You must be willing and able to spend time training and playing with your pet bird.

Is My Home Suitable?

Although their cages may be small, birds need room to fly around. It is important to ensure your pet bird gets enough exercise. Your home must also be bird-friendly. Keep in mind the needs of your bird and your family. Is your sibling or parent allergic to feathers? Do you have other pets to think about? Birds can be fun, but their songs or screams may be loud and disruptive to other family members. Finding the right fit is crucial for you and your pet.

Life Cycle

You can buy your pet bird from a pet store or a bird breeder. If you like, you can even raise your pet bird from an egg all the way to adulthood. Birds have different requirements at varying stages in their development. It is important to learn what your bird's needs are, so you can properly care for him.

Eggs and Hatching

When an adult bird lays eggs, they must be kept warm. Sitting on the eggs helps protect them. It also provides warmth to help the baby bird inside grow. Do not move or touch a bird's egg before it hatches. This can harm the bird inside. Germs from your hands may pass through the egg's shell. After two to six weeks, the baby bird will break through the shell using his beak.

Maturity

Several birds are considered adults within a few months to 1 year. Others are not fully grown until they reach 2 or 3 years of age. Adult birds shed their feathers and grow new ones. This is called molting. Molting can be very stressful for your pet bird. Try to keep your molting bird comfortable with lots of baths and fresh water.

Chicks

Some breeds of chicks have feathers. They are able to feed on their own and move around shortly after hatching. Other breeds are born featherless and blind. They are totally dependent. After two weeks, most chicks are covered in **down**. Some may even have wing feathers. It is important to be gentle when handling a chick. He may need help to balance at first.

Fledglings

When a chick begins to develop flight feathers, he is called a fledgling. Although they begin to explore their surroundings at this stage, fledglings still depend on their parents to feed them. You must be careful not to interfere too much with fledglings. Some birds will abandon their babies if they are handled by humans.

It is important to clean your bird's cage, food bowl, and water dish on a regular basis.

Bird Basics

When you buy your pet bird, she will need some basic supplies. Make sure that you have everything you need to keep your bird safe and comfortable.

Your bird's cage must be large enough for her to move around in, especially if you do not take her out to exercise. Be careful to arrange the items in your bird's cage properly. Her food bowl should be placed away from where her droppings may fall.

You can include a perch for your bird to help keep her feet healthy. Be mindful of sandpaper perches. These do wear down overgrown claws, but can also hurt your bird's feet. A feeder may also be useful. This will allow food to drop into a tray, as your bird needs it.

Birds love to chew, so provide your pet with some toys. No part of the cage or the items inside should be breakable or toxic. Night-lights can be used to calm birds who may be scared of the dark.

Another way to keep your home bird-friendly is to close toilet lids. Your bird may try to take a drink from the toilet bowl, which can be dangerous. Also ensure that your bird's cage is secure. You do not want her to escape and possibly injure herself. It is important to protect your bird from accidental harm.

Birds eat a variety of foods, depending on their species. A bird's diet can include seeds, nuts, fruit, vegetables, or meat.

Eating Like a Bird

Depending on your bird's breed, he will require different types of foods. Your bird will also need fresh drinking water every day. Certain human foods can be dangerous for birds. Never feed a bird avocados, chocolate, or salty snacks. These can be poisonous to birds.

How Much Should I Feed My Bird?

A bird will need different amounts of food at various stages of his life. Birds that are very active need more food. The majority of birds eat small meals throughout the day. Your pet bird should never go without eating for hours at a time. Your **veterinarian** can tell you what foods are most suitable for your pet bird and when you should feed him.

What if My Bird Is Picky?

Some birds can be fussy eaters. This may be due to stubbornness. However, it may also mean your bird is sick. Pay close attention to your bird's eating habits. This will help you detect when your bird is ill. When your bird is molting, he may need extra vitamins. Grit can also help your bird's digestion. Grit is made of small sand and shell particles. Always ask your veterinarian for advice on proper feeding of your pet bird.

From Feathers to Feet

Birds are unique because of their feathers. They are the only creatures that have them. Birds also have hollow bones. Their skeletons are sturdy, but lightweight. Special air sacs help birds breathe much more quickly than other animals. These features, combined with their strong wing muscles, are what enable birds to fly.

Beak

A bird's beak is made of bone and **keratin**. It is used for **preening**, eating, and sometimes even climbing.

Eyes

Many birds have eyes located on the sides of their heads. Each eye is protected by three eyelids.

Head

Most birds are capable of turning their heads 180 degrees.

Air Sacs

Birds have nine air sacs. These help to regulate body temperature and allow birds to breathe high in the sky.

Contour Feathers

A bird's contour feathers give it a distinct shape. They can be found on the tail, wings, and body.

Legs

Birds have two strong legs. They are protected by scales.

Tail

The tail controls direction when a bird is flying. It also helps with landings.

Claws

In nature, birds use their claws to capture **prey**. Domestic birds need their claws to help grip their perch.

Birds preen their feathers to keep them smooth. A bird's beak acts as a zipper, closing the sections of each feather.

Bird Bath

To keep your bird clean, make sure she is able to bathe regularly. Put a bowl of water in your bird's cage for her to splash around in. Be careful not to fill it too high. Birds can drown in a very small amount of water. You can also mist your bird with water from a spray bottle. This acts like a shower, which many birds enjoy.

Your bird will also preen herself to keep clean. This is done with her beak. Your bird uses oil from a gland at the base of her tail to preen. Preening is very important for your pet bird. It keeps her feathers waterproof, and also removes dirt and **parasites**.

You should also keep your bird's claws trimmed. This can be quite difficult, so you should let your veterinarian show you the best method. You may need to wear gloves or use a small towel to protect yourself from scratches.

Healthy birds will have clean, shiny feathers. Your bird may also need to have her wings trimmed. This task can cause serious injury to your bird if done incorrectly. Only your veterinarian should perform this task.

Before letting your bird out of its cage, be sure the area is safe. All doors and windows should be closed. Fans should be turned off. Any sharp or dangerous items should be removed.

Birds need **toys** to keep their minds active and healthy. Birds should have as many as **10** to **14** toys in their cages.

Your bird's **cage** should be at least **two** to **three** times the width of his **wingspan**. This allows him enough space to move around.

If a bird loses **5 percent** of his total body weight, it could be a sign of a serious **health condition**.

Healthy and Happy

Choose the right spot for your bird's cage to be placed. It should not be too close to the television, because birds are anxious around loud noises. Make sure to keep the cage away from extreme heat, drafts, or direct sunlight as well. It is not safe to keep your bird's cage in the kitchen. The fumes from cleaning products or cooking can make your bird sick.

If your bird will be free flying in your home, check to see if the room is safe. Cover all mirrors and windows with curtains or decals. This will prevent your bird from crashing into them. You should also close all doors and windows so that your bird stays in the area where you want him to fly. Remove anything that could be dangerous for your bird. This includes food, plants, or ornaments. It is important to ensure your bird has a safe space to fly. This will give him the exercise he needs, and prevent boredom.

You should check your bird's appearance frequently, and monitor his behavior. Are his droppings normal? Does he have tattered feathers? Has he stopped singing? These may all be symptoms that something is wrong. Talk to your veterinarian if your bird acts out of the ordinary. Take your bird for regular checkups, and treat him when he is ill or hurt.

In some bird species, males are more likely to learn to talk than females. Treats can be used to reward talking.

Bird Behavior

It takes patience to teach your bird to talk. You should make sure there are no distractions around, such as other birds or people. It is easier for your bird to have only one teacher. Start with simple words, such as "Hi, birdie." Repeat them every time you pass your bird's cage.

As your bird learns how to speak, it will become easier for her to pick up new words. Talk to your pet bird often. This will encourage her to talk back.

Some birds are better at speaking than others. Parrots and mynas are among the best bird talkers. A parrot from England was able to say almost 800 different words. This may be because the part of the brain that controls learning is larger in parrots than in other birds. The earlier in life you start teaching your pet bird to talk, the better she will become at speaking.

Tweety cartoons featured
Sylvester the Cat in
every episode after 1947.

Above and Beyond

Throughout history, humans have appreciated birds. It is because of birds that people have dreamed of soaring through the sky. This dream of freedom led to the invention of the modern airplane. An airplane's wings are modeled after a bird's wings.

Some very well-known people have been bird lovers. President Thomas Jefferson owned a pet bird during his time in the White House. Named Dick, this pet mockingbird went with the president wherever he went. Dick would sit on Jefferson's shoulder as his faithful companion.

Birds also appear as characters or **symbols** in stories and legends. For example, doves are a symbol of peace. Several stories tell of a dove being released and returning with an olive branch. This meant that suffering had ended, or that a war was over. Ancient legends explain that witches could transform into any kind of bird, except a dove.

Other popular stories about birds come in the form of television shows or movies. One of the most recognizable characters in cartoon history is Tweety, a little yellow canary featured in many Warner Brothers cartoons. Tweety first appeared on television in 1942.

Pet Puzzlers

What do you know about birds? If you can answer the following questions correctly, you may be ready to own a bird.

1 How many pet birds are there in the United States?

2 What were canaries used for during World War II?

3 How do cockatiels use the crests on their heads?

4 What is the average life span of a parakeet?

5 What should you do if your pet bird acts out?

6 Why is it important not to handle fledglings?

7 What do birds eat?

8 How many eyelids do birds have?

9 How big should your bird's cage be?

10 What should you avoid when placing your bird's cage?

Bird Calls

Before you bring home your pet bird, brainstorm some bird names you like. Some names may work better for a female bird. Others may suit a male bird. Here are just a few suggestions.

Buddy

Peeps

Glider

Ginger

Daisy

Dolly

Howie

Tweety

Pipes

Key Words

breed: a group of animals that shares specific characteristics

crests: tufts of feathers on a bird's head

domesticated: tamed and made to live among people

down: soft fur covering a baby chick

fossils: remains of animals and plants from long ago, found in rocks

keratin: the same strong substance found in human fingernails

parasites: organisms that live on or in other organisms to obtain nutrients

perches: elevated poles or rods for birds to roost on

preening: using the beak to groom by arranging and cleaning feathers

prey: animals that are hunted and eaten by other animals

symbols: items used to stand in for and represent things, feelings, and ideas

veterinarian: animal doctor

veterinary: medical treatment of animals

Index

Get the best of both worlds.

AV2 bridges the gap between print and digital.

The expandable resources toolbar enables quick access to content including **videos**, **audio**, **activities**, **weblinks**, **slideshows**, **quizzes**, and **key words**.

Animated videos make static images come alive.

Resource icons on each page help readers to further **explore key concepts**.

Published by AV2
350 5th Avenue, 59th Floor
New York, NY 10118
Website: www.av2books.com

Library of Congress Cataloging-in-Publication Data

Names: Hamilton, Lynn, 1964- author. | Gillespie, Katie, author.
Title: Bird / Lynn Hamilton and Katie Gillespie.
Description: New York, NY : AV2 by Weigl, [2020] | Series: Pets we love |
Includes index. | Audience: Grades 4-6 |
Identifiers: LCCN 2019048004 (print) | LCCN 2019048005 (ebook) | ISBN
9781791119089 (library binding) | ISBN 9781791119096 (library binding) | ISBN 9781791119102 (ebook other) | ISBN 9781791119119 (ebook other)
Subjects: LCSH: Cage birds--Juvenile literature.
Classification: LCC SF461.35 .H348 2020 (print) | LCC SF461.35 (ebook) |
DDC 636.6/8--dc23
LC record available at https://lccn.loc.gov/2019048004
LC ebook record available at https://lccn.loc.gov/2019048005

Printed in Guangzhou, China
1 2 3 4 5 6 7 8 9 0   24 23 22 21 20

022020
101319

Project Coordinator Sara Cucini
Art Director Terry Paulhus

Photo Credits
Every reasonable effort has been made to trace ownership and to obtain permission to reprint copyright material. The publishers would be pleased to have any errors or omissions brought to their attention so that they may be corrected in subsequent printings. AV2 acknowledges Getty Images, Alamy, and Shutterstock as its primary photo suppliers for this title.